Copyright © 2021 by Marcella Morse
Published by Marcella Morse

Angels on Earth

Written and Illustrated
by
Marcella Morse

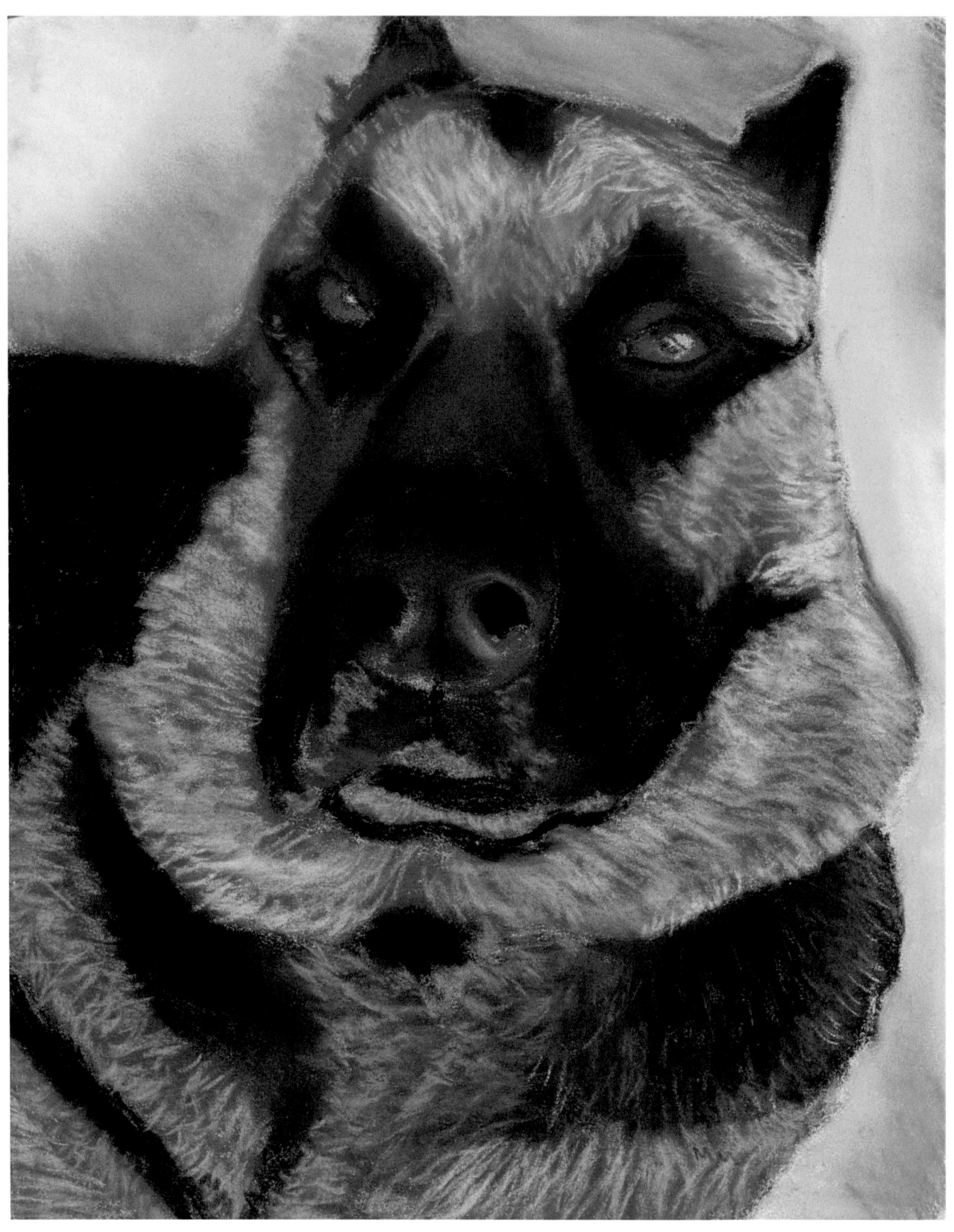

Angels on earth is when you see love through their eyes.

It's when you come home feeling joy in your heart.

When you go to sleep at night knowing someone is by your side.

Waking up every morning with a big smile on your face.

Walking outside knowing you're not alone.

Guiding you when you can't see.

Finding things that you can't find.

Staying with you when you're ill.

Waiting for you to come home.

Protecting your secrets from other people.

Making dining experience fun.

Being a sidekick in your car.

Having a vacuum cleaner when you don't feel like cleaning up.

Saving lives that you can't save.

Keeping an eye on you in the kitchen.

Being a bodyguard when you need one.

Teaching things that you can't teach.

Forgiving you for your mistakes.

Listening to you while you are speaking.

Telling you something is wrong.

Helping you when you need help.

Having a childhood friend forever.

These are the type of angels that have tails with four legs with a big capacity for unconditional love to give us. And even if you don't see them anymore you know they are still with you because you can feel them in your heart.

www.ingramcontent.com/pod-product-compliance
Lightning Source LLC
Chambersburg PA
CBRC102059150426
43192CB00005B/126